How I Made
$5,400 ON AIRBNB IN 7 DAYS

7 Easy Steps

By:
Nichola Dotson
5 Star Airbnb Host

Introduction

Hi, I'm Nichola Dotson! Thank you for downloading this ebook. First let's look at my recent earnings.

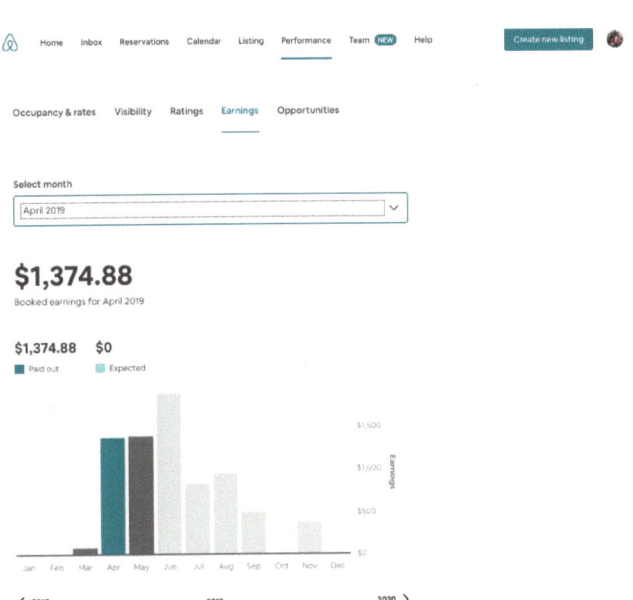

Occupancy & rates   Visibility   Ratings   **Earnings**   Opportunities

Select month

| May 2019 | ∨ |

$1,390.89
Booked earnings for May 2019

$1,390.89   **$0**
■ Paid out   ■ Expected

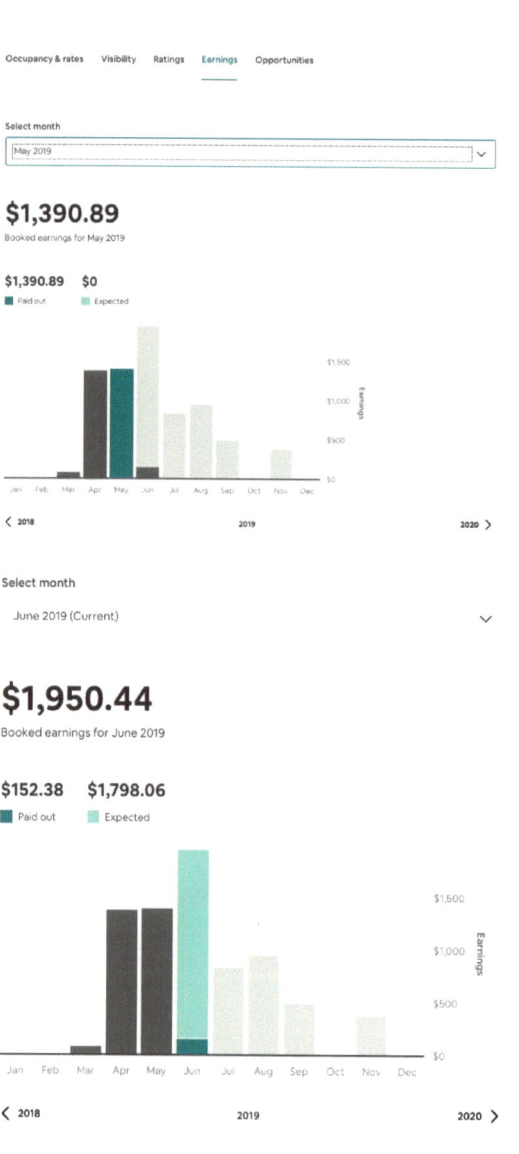

‹ 2018   2019   2020 ›

Select month

June 2019 (Current)   ∨

$1,950.44
Booked earnings for June 2019

$152.38   **$1,798.06**
■ Paid out   ■ Expected

‹ 2018   2019   2020 ›

On the previous pages you saw my earnings from the past few months and a glance of what has already been put on the books for the rest of the year. We started with proof so we could cut straight to the chase. You want to learn how to make money on Airbnb? I want to show you how I am doing it! I'm a Landlord Entrepreneur who specializes in Real Estate Investing, Property Management, Customer Service and Marketing. I am also a wife and my most precious title a mother of 3 sons. As of late, I have been moonlighting as a 5 star rated Airbnb Host.

Now that you've seen the money let me start by saying I stumbled into becoming an Airbnb Host. I purchased a 4 unit apartment building near Frankenmuth, MI in late 2017 that needed a lot of TLC. In the midst of me renovating one of the units, my sister asked me if I'd ever considered hosting on Airbnb, I hadn't. She thought I could possibly make money hosting on Airbnb to help me fund my Real Estate projects. Great idea!

This wasn't the first time I'd heard about Airbnb, I'd stayed in one before my friends used Airbnb often and one of my friends was already a host and had 4 Airbnb rentals already. Airbnb is the Uber/Lyft for homes! I decided to reach out to my friend who is also in Real Estate to ask him about his Airbnb business. A short conversation led me to some research of my own. Turned out that I was actually in a pretty hot spot for tourism and there was money to be made in my area with my apartment so I decided to renovate one unit specifically for Airbnb and give it a shot. What's the worst that could happen? I figured at worst I would quit hosting and just rent it out to a permanent tenant like originally planned I only had money to gain!

I own a virtual call center which only had two employees, my husband and I. We use to provide professional client support service for Fortune 100 companies on a contractual basis. Around the same time I wanted to try

Airbnb, I received an email offer for my virtual call center to provide services for Airbnb. Coincidence? I think NOT! Instead, saw it as a sign.

Took the contract for my virtual call center with one purpose in mind, see if they were as awesome as a company as they appeared to be because this was uncharted territory for me. Went through Airbnb's employee training then started answering calls from host and guest of Airbnb as a customer service agent. Working around my apartment building renovation, I listened to the host and guest, learned from the host and guest, absorbed everything I could from the host and guest and that experience made me a believer!

So much excitement everyday to finish my renovation because I was so eager to go live and start hosting guest on Airbnb. Totally obsessed with the idea Airbnb had to make everyone feel like they belonged I wanted to be apart of this amazing community Airbnb had created. I work so much so I don't get out a lot to make new friends, I liked that I could possibly make new friends with people who wanted to stay in my apartment. The possibilities were endless and I was excited.

I expected to see some success (I always expect to succeed!) But I didn't expect to start getting bookings within minutes after going live! I didn't expect to generate over $5400 in income on the Airbnb platform within my first week. I didn't expect to have to quit my call center gig so quickly! My first month I got PAID $1374 but I put $5400 on the calendar within my first 7 days of going live! One of my guest let me know they will be needing their unit for the rest of the year but, at the time she booked, my booking settings where only set to 45 days maximum stay. She didn't let me know until later that she needed an apartment until the end of the year. I have since updated this setting because I love long term Airbnber's but I have also started renovating a second unit to accommodate the guest when her 45 days is up. So technically, one Unit was booked for the rest of the year within the first month. That money is not even accounted for in the proof you saw above. I was so sold and so obsessed with the results and the experience that I changed my entire Real Estate Investing plan.

60 Days Later, 22 and counting 5 star reviews you see my progress. I have all the basics, now part of the work collection and on track to becoming a Superhost. I have been booked since I started hosting and I still get inquires

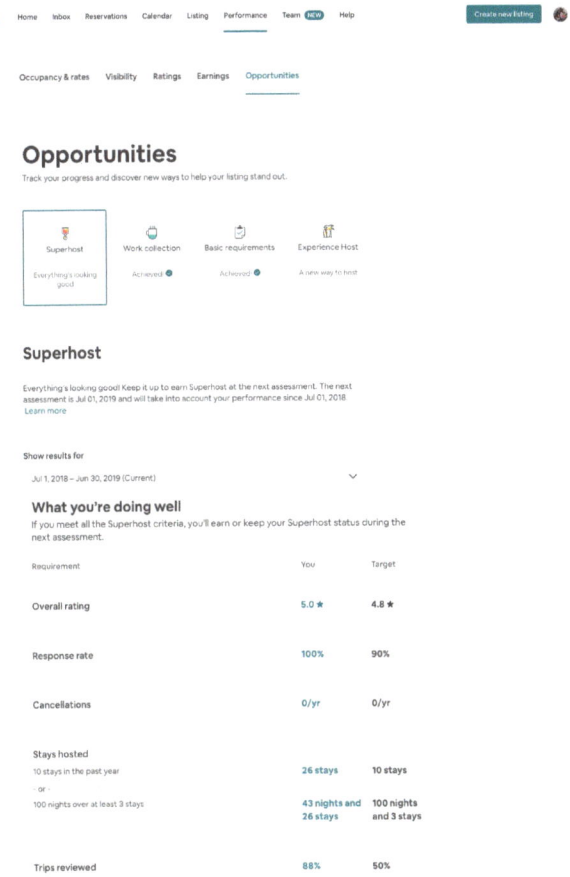

about dates that are already booked. Who knows how many people have to turn away after seeing I am BOOKED after viewing my calendar. There is money to be made on Airbnb and I have created this book to show you how to get ahold of yours! My Occupancy Rate VS Average Occupancy Rate of host in my area

Occupancy rate by listing

Listing

 Modern Luxury Near Frankenmuth Amazing Beds & XBOX

Occupancy rate ⑦   Market average ⑦

100%   43%

There is a 57% difference between me and my competitors. That means I earn 57% MORE than my entire market

That means While I make $1300-$1900 on average per month my market is making $559-$817 on average per month

That is a jaw dropping $741-$1083 pay difference between me and my market. The information in this book will tell you how I did it and how I continue to do it!

Step 1:Research
Who? What? When? Where? How? And Why?

Before you go any further, first check out some statistics about Airbnb

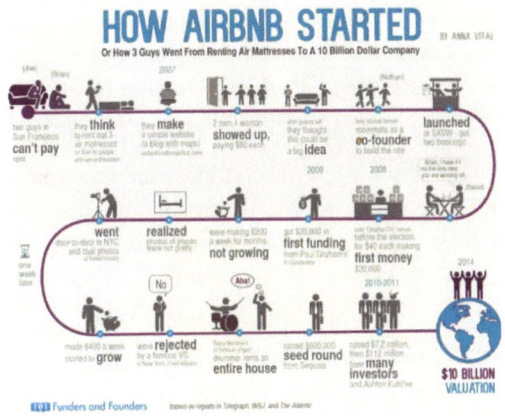

Airbnb has about 150 million users

In the last decade, Airbnb has come a long way in terms of user base, coverage, and revenue. When it launched in 2008, it had zero bookings and I can boldly say there's zero interest at the time.

Fast forward today and more than 260 million guests have booked and stayed in Airbnb properties across the world. A recent statistics show that Airbnb has approximately 150 million users covering more than 65,000 cities. Guests can also book 1.9 million listings at any given time. It started small but it's grown significantly since then. Check out all sorts of statistics and fun facts about Airbnb here: **muchneeded.com/airbnb-statistics/**

Who is your guest? Why do people travel to your town? What is special about your neighborhood? LOCATION LOCATION LOCATION! Do people come to your city for business? Do you live near campus where professors or student parents may frequent in your area? Maybe you live down the street from an amusement park, first let's think about our location.

Figuring out why someone may need to stay at your place is the first thing you should research and figure out. Why waste time crafting a summer vibe villa if you live near a ski resort? Who is our guest is the first mission to solve. Ask yourself, Why would my guest be in town? About how old are they? What things are there to do around me? Will my guest likely need 1 night or long term stays? What type of amenities will they need? What amenities will they want that they can't get somewhere else?

Once you know who your guest is (which wants and needs will vary) you can create an experience just for them!

Example: My guest most likely are traveling for tourism with family, work alone or business partner or a quick getaway. My husband and I work from home ourselves so we wanted to create a space functional for work, family with children and couple getaways. I provide stainless steel appliances, TV, Wi-Fi, Desk, Dining table, fully stocked kitchen, washer/dryer with detergent, plush and firm mattresses, coffee, tea and some food items.

I recommend creating a space organic to your lifestyle or an experience your guest would be delighted to stay for the night or forever! Even if they can't stay forever you want them to feel like they'd want to.

Now let's get into the MONEY that's what we are here for right? First let's go over some basics.

1 Twin Size Bed	=	1 Adult Guest or Possibly 2 small children
1 Full Size Bed	=	1 Adult Guest Or 2 Children
1 Queen Size Bed	=	2 Adult Guest
1 King Size Bed	=	2 Adult Guest
1 Large Sofa	=	1 Adult Guest
Large Sectional	=	2 Adult guest
2 Large Sofas	=	2 Adult guest

Based off of this table, how many guest can your home, private room or shared room accommodate? This is important for our next step to estimating how much money you can make on Airbnb with your space. I have a 2 Bedroom Apartment, each bedroom has a queen sized bed (I handmade to save money) and the living room has a large sofa. Therefore my space accommodates 5 guest. Of course sometimes there are more because they have small children or elder parents but I don't charge for extra guest because my space is family friendly and I let guest decide how comfortable their family is and how they choose to sleep. No need to nit-pick on the small stuff. Now that you know how many guest your space can accommodate use this link to see how much money Airbnb can guarantee you monthly based on how many guest you can host.

Use this custom link: WWW.AIRBNB.COM/R/JKLHOMESREFERRAL

Input your city and state, in the drop down select how many guest you can accommodate, select either Entire Home, Private Rooms or Shared Rooms and it will automatically update the Monthly earning potential for you.

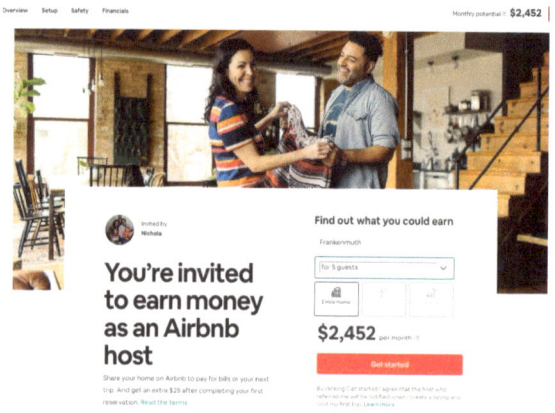

Play with this if you can add more guest accommodations get an estimate for how many guest you'd like to host in the future as well. This earnings estimate assumes 15 nights booked per month at forecasted daily prices. The forecasted daily prices are based on average prices for listings with a similar location, listing type, and guest capacity. How much you actually make may vary with your pricing, type and location of your listing, actual occupancy rate, season, demand, local laws, and other factors.If you do decide to click Get Started and create your free host profile you will get an extra $25 after completing your first reservation just because you used my link to get started. Glad you have this book now? I have already made you $25!

Now that you have seen your income potential you should know now if you'd like to continue. I recommend searching for listings in your area as if you were a guest to see what other hosts are doing well and even learn from the hosts who are not doing so well and read their guest compliments/complaints. Get as much information as you can about your area. Learn what guest like and also what guest don't like and think about ideas that can make sure you stand apart. I am sure you will notice that some listings look better than others and I will get to that later in this book but, for now let's talk more about your space.

Here is the link to my listing: www.airbnb.com/rooms/27966512

Step 2: Select Your Space
Entire Home, Private Rooms or Shared Rooms?

Will you be listing an entire home, private rooms or shared rooms? This is entirely up to you. Are you okay with sharing your homes common spaces with a stranger? Would you like everyone to have their own apartment? Travel for work a lot or rarely home? You can host only when you are away and make sure the guest stays only last while you are away. You are in complete control of how often you get booked. There are settings available that allow you set minimum and maximum amount of days a guest can stay. You can also block off specific days in your calendar to make sure you are only hosting guest when it's convenient for you. How often do you want to turnover the space? Or, how often you want to pay someone else to turnover the space for you are great things to consider while budgeting. We will get to budgeting later.

If you choose the private rooms route I recommend putting keypad door knobs on your bedroom doors because it creates a sense of security for the guest and most importantly YOU as the host. Keypad door knobs keep your personal belongings behind your secure bedroom door even when you are not home and when you sleep at night you know there is no one coming into your bedroom.

I own a 4-unit apartment building with a main front entrance, back entrance and each apartment has their own personal door entry within the building. I use Kwikset and Defiant brands for my Keypad Deadbolts both which I purchased from Home Depot. If you can wait, Amazon carries the same products and most times at a better price. But depending on how I decide to run my Airbnb business in the future, I may convert to keypad locks that allow me to add and delete codes from my iPhone.

Here are a few options:

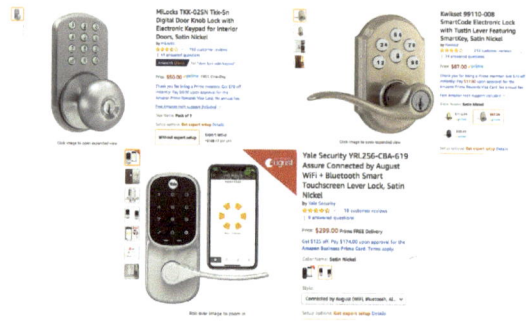

I have deadbolt keypads on front and back building entrances but I only set the front main entrance up with Airbnb Guest codes and my instructions let them know to only use the front main entrance. I also set the same code I give the guest for their apartment entry code. I usually set the code up to be the last 4 digits of the phone number listed in the guest profile they used to book my apartment. This is also an extra layer of security because everyone should know the last 4 digits of their own phone number if they are who they say they are right?

Self check-in is a very sought after amenity. Some guest like the idea of this easy check-in option because this means their chances of being locked out because the host is not physically available to let them in because they are later than expected are slim to none. One less stress the guest has to worry about therefore some guest ONLY search for listings that have Self check-in and that is where you want to be in order to make the most money you can in your area.

Here are some of the amenities a guest may select while searching. These are also the amenities I currently offer. You want to make the most money you can in your area right? Self check-in is an amenity you MUST have to accomplish that!

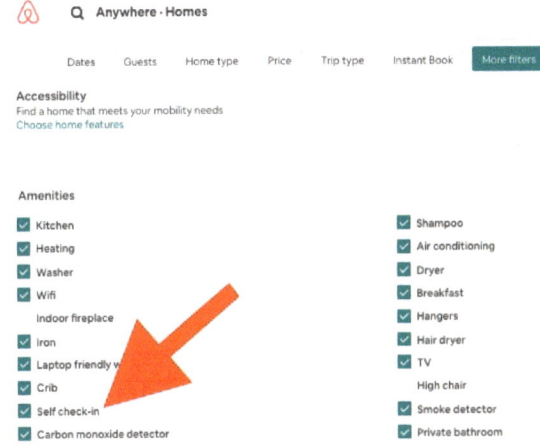

Step 3: Select Your Guest (Niche)
Family Friendly? Work Travelers? Or Something Else?

Is your space family kid friendly? Great for date night? Or ideal for business travelers? I setup our Airbnb to be comfortable and functional for a working family, work travelers and date night! If you looked at my listing you saw that I provide desk, dining table, wi-fi, TV, Xbox One, Chalkboard (for the kiddos), puzzles, fully stocked kitchen, washer/dryer and more. I wanted my guest to have everything they would need to feel more at home from the moment they walk-in and see a sign next to their door that welcomes them by name until they go to sleep in an amazing bed at night with an inspirational pillow. I recommend creating a space or experience that is easy for you to put your personal touch on.

If your place is ideal for families then your amenities should include TV either cable or with apps like Netflix, Amazon Prime, HBO , etc., should be available whether you have a smart tv or you have a device like an Apple TV that can turn your TV into a smart tv. Whatever you do PROVIDE television.

If you can provide a game console families LOVE that, I cannot tell you how many people have told me they have booked me for the XBOX One alone. The families who have booked with me have loved the ability to wash and dry their own clothes while in the apartment. I provide pot, pans, cooking utensils and seasonings to make meal preparation for a family easy. One guest told me she always wanted to cook in a kitchen like mines and then she cooked all night. Think about what your guest may need and want then take it up a notch and level up their experience. You get the 5 star ratings by providing exceptional SERVICE, SERVICE is how you stand apart. If you don't have a lot of money to invest in TV's right now, consider a rent to own option like Aaron but make sure your budget not only covers the cost but also still gives you a profit.

If you would like to attract business travelers and join the work collection this is what you MUST have: www.airbnb.com/help/article/2186/how-do-i-join-the-work-collection

How do I join the work collection?

We'll automatically add your listing to the work collection if it meets certain eligibility criteria and requirements. To track your eligibility and requirements, go to Progress.

Listing and property type

We've limited the work collection to types of listings we think business travelers will love. Your listing must be classified as: an entire home, a private room with a private bath, or a private room with an ensuite bath. Eligible property types include: house, apartment, bungalow, cabin, chalet, townhouse, villa, guesthouse, loft, condo, hotel, or bed and breakfast.

Amenities

Your listing must offer the following amenities:

- Essentials (toilet paper, soap, towels, bed linens, and pillows)
- Self check-in (a key lockbox, keypad, smartlock, or by getting the key or access from a doorperson or front desk attendant)
- Wifi
- TV
- Iron
- Hair dryer
- Hangers
- Shampoo
- Laptop-friendly workspace
- Carbon monoxide detector
- Smoke detector

Reviews and response rate

Your listing must maintain a 4.8 overall rating or higher in the past 365 days, with 5 or more reviews. You must also maintain an average check-in rating of 4.8 or higher.

Hosts of listings that are good for work trips also must have responded to 90% of booking requests within 24 hours over the last year.

Cancellations

Your listing must offer a flexible or moderate cancellation policy.

Eligibility

Once your listing meets these requirements, it will automatically be added to the work collection. Keep in mind that you'll need to continue to meet each requirement in order to stay in the collection.

Airbnb may update or change the requirements to qualify for collections at any time. By participating in a collection, you agree to be subject to any applicable terms and criteria. Airbnb reserves the right to change any collections, or their terms and criteria, at any time.

Also, all hosts on Airbnb are expected to follow our basic requirements for hosts.

Step 4: Budget, Plan and Design
Big budget or no budget? Either way we PLAN!

First and foremost we need to determine a real dollar amount you are able to invest to get your space ready to be listed on Airbnb. Maybe you have everything you need maybe you don't! Either way you have options.

On the next page I have a budget template for you.

Airbnb Cost	Price Range Upfront	Cost Per Month	Have (Put $0)	I Want or Need
Keypad Locks	$49 - $300	$0		
Paint (DIY or Hire)	$30 - $100 1 Can of Paint or per hour if hiring a painter	$0		
Sofa/Love Seat	$0 - $1400 If you buy	$100-300 If renting		
Television	$0 — $600 If you own or buy new	$50 - $200 If renting		
Cable TV/TV Apps Memberships	$0 - $100/month Most you can start a free trial	$10-$80		
Game Console/ Memberships	$0 - $300	$0 -$60		
Desk/Chair	$0 - $40	$0		
Dining Table/Chairs	$0 - $89	$0		
Water/Coffee/Tea/ Oatmeal/Grits	$20	$20 - $50 This is based on you will provide		
Kitchen Essentials	$0 - $150	$0-30 You should update and add as you host more		
Household Cleaning Supplies/Detergents	$50	$50		
Towels/Linens	$0 - $200	$30		
Mattres/Pillow covers	$10-$200+	$0		
Utility Bills	$0 - $99	$20-$150+		
Maid Services (I clean)	$0 — $100 each cleaning	$0-$400+		
Professional Photography	$50 - $200	$0		
Listing Management Services	$0 - $49	10%-20% Of Booked Revenue Earnings		
Totals		Add these	$	$
Final Startup Cost				

Your space may already be ready to list, if so congratulations use my link to sign up as a host and get going! WWW.AIRBNB.COM/R/JKLHOMESREFERRAL If you are not ready and have little to no money, you are going to need to rely heavily on creativity, craigslist, garage sales and/or family and friends to help you get your space ready.

If you have somewhat of a budget and only need to get a few things to make your space ideal, Ikea, Amazon and Walmart are probably going to become your new best friends. Here are some of the things I purchased to make my place more modern and functional.

I got my modern looking Dining table and chairs from Ikea for $89. It came with a table and 4 chairs.

Here is the link: https://www.ikea.com/us/en/catalog/products/S79010690/

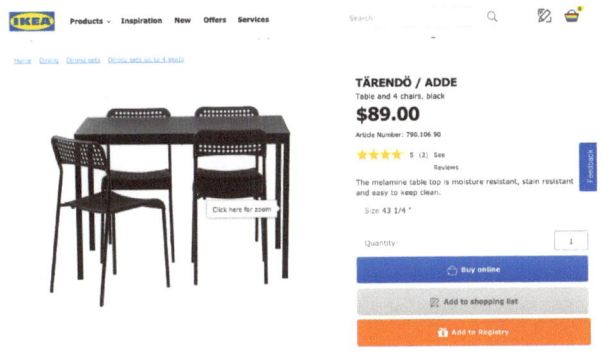

The sofa I use in the Airbnb is one part from a very large sectional I purchased for my personal home, I was able to separate it and still have a small sectional left for me in my home so it cost me nothing for a sofa.

I have Xbox and magazines on floating shelf from Ikea for $30.

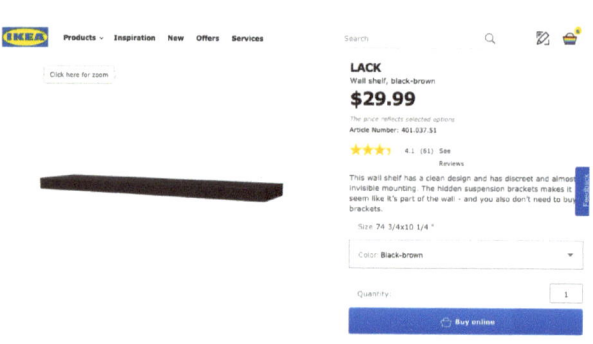

I got my desk and chair also from Ikea for under $40.

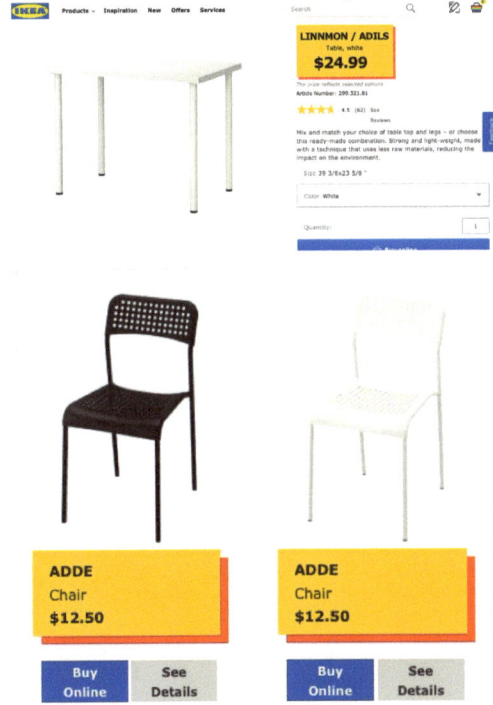

I got 2 sets of Duvet Covers and Pillowcases from Ikea $12.99 each but I purchased other sets still brand new in the box at Goodwill for less than $15 each as well. Amazon has really great options for Duvet Cover sets as well. You use Duvet Covers to cover your comforter for easier turnover so instead of washing the actual comforter each time a guest check out you can just remove the duvet cover put the comforter in dryer for 20 minutes or steam it and replace it with a clean duvet cover. Even if you have to use the same duvet cover it's easier to wash over washing a full comforter because they are just heavier than duvet covers and sheets. Makes being able to wash sheets, pillowcases and duvet covers at the same time a breeze for turnover. I wash towels separately. I currently have 6 sets total for a two bedroom apartment and I got to 6 by starting with 2 and adding one or two at a time as the money came.

Home   Bedroom   Bedding   Duvet cover sets

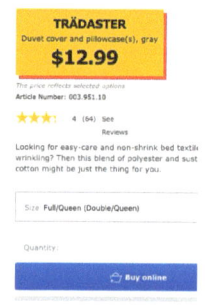

TRÄDASTER
Duvet cover and pillowcase(s), gray
$12.99

The price reflects selected options
Article Number: 003.951.10

★★★☆ 4 (64) See
Reviews

Looking for easy-care and non-shrink bed textile
wrinkling? Then this blend of polyester and sust
cotton might be just the thing for you.

Size Full/Queen (Double/Queen)

Quantity:

🛒 Buy online

Also a helpful tip, if you buy all your linens in the same color group you can wash more things together at once. I prefer all white or mostly white linens and towels.I bought my towels from Walmart because they look nice really fluffy and feel awesome when you get out the shower but, they don't break the bank!

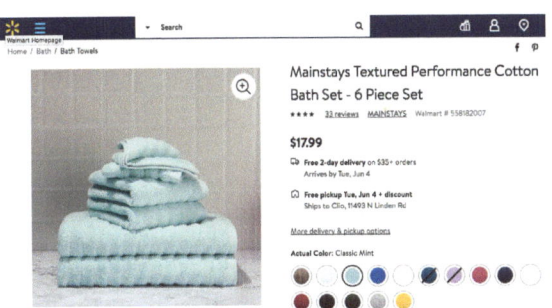

I got inspiring wall stickers from the Dollar Tree. The Dollar Tree also has great plates, bowls, saucers, coffee mugs and glassware everything a dollar a piece. I got my Dinnerware set from Ikea: www.ikea.com/us/en/catalog/categories/departments/eating/31781/

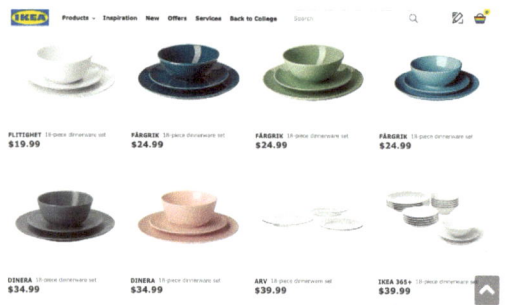

Now that you have a better idea of how much income you can make per month but also how much it will cost you to startup and run your Airbnb business, you can play with your budget and remember everything doesn't have to be available right away. As long as you are honest in your listing about what you do provide and never mislead the guest you will still get bookings.

I clean my own Airbnb but if you would like to research pricing check out https://www.tidy.com/cleaning-service-pricing/

Step 5: Safety and Security
Is it safe? YES

Biggest question I hear all the time, is it safe? I heard from my friend who is not an Airbnb host that this whole thing was just unsafe! Technically driving a car isn't safe but that doesn't stop us from getting in it and driving to the grocery store now do we? I didn't think so. Obviously keeping you safe is priority number one, which is why you have already decided if you will be sharing a space with a guest or not and if so which precautions you'd like in place!

You can take extra precautions to keep you safe. You can set more requirements such as making it a requirement that guest provide valid identification to Airbnb and be verified before they can book with you. You can also set your listing up for guest to first request to book with you so you can look at your potential guest profile to see their reviews or get to know them some before you accept or decline their reservation. You have more control of who stays in your listing than you think.

I HIGHLY recommend you DO NOT use this as a way to discriminate against people because Airbnb doesn't not take that lightly and YOU WILL be kicked off the platform not being able to list again if you do. Remember Airbnb is about making EVERYONE feel like they belong. I have a feature called Instant Book whereas long as they have valid ID and at least 1 good review they can instantly book my listing without it coming to me for a review. I get request to book request from others who may be new to the platform but I have never declined a booking request because I don't live in the apartment listed and I feel safe within my home I don't really care what the person looks like if they are new what they are doing here every day they are booked I just don't care about those things.

Airbnb also has a messaging system that allows you to message your guest ask questions and get to know your guest before they arrive. You are also empowered to set your house rules that the guest must agree to while booking. You can set restrictions on smoking and parties. If your guest violates your rules you cancel their reservation.

In the rare case of property damage, Airbnb's Host Guarantee provides free protection of up to $1,000,000 USD in property damage for every booking, every time. Claims can be filed directly through our Resolution Center.

Airbnb also provides free Host Protection Insurance covering liability claims up to $1,000,000 USD. This insurance is for the unlikely event that someone files a lawsuit or claim against you for bodily injury or property damage that occurs in a listing, or on your property, during a stay.

Airbnb support is available 24/7 to support you and your guests by phone, email, and live chat you are never in this alone.

If you will be sharing a space I recommend you have a safe for your personal belongings and also keypad locks on bedroom doors as I stated earlier. I like keypad entry doors because I never have to worry about someone making a key and coming back, I delete all user codes each time a guest checks out. I set the expectation that I do not disturb guest and like to give them privacy but only a text away should an issue arise.

Step 6: Listing Your Space

Photos and Descriptions Matter, Cleaning and how to get great reviews

40%
increase in earnings

Hosts with professional photos tend to earn
more than other hosts in their area.

26%
higher nightly price

Many hosts are able to raise their nightly
price after upgrading their photos.

24%
more bookings

Photos are one of the top reasons guests
choose to book.

I highly recommend you hiring a local real estate photographer to come out and shoot your listing before you list on Airbnb. I cannot express the importance of beautiful photos enough. I cannot express enough the importance of using professional photos. These numbers are based on a 2016 study of more than 100,000 listings with and without professional photography.

First impressions matter! Find a photographer! We are talking about earning the most you can right out the gate so we are talking professional photos. My photos are absolutely responsible for getting bookings the same day I went live! My host profile was already setup long before I created my first listing and my profile was verified before becoming a host so keep in mind that Airbnb may need to verify you and your listing before you going live just in case you have to wait for a verifying period before your listing showing up live on Airbnb.

I am not going to sugar coat this, creating a listing may only take you a few hours or an entire day or a few days or a few weeks it truly depends on the person.

What you need:

1. Captivating title

2. Summary

3. Description of your property

4. Things to do nearby

5. House rules

6. Select all of your amenities, be honest

7. Setup your calendar, block important dates now

8. Set your pricing, I recommend smart pricing

9. Setup all of your settings

Airbnb's platform does make it fairly simple to navigate. If you feel you would prefer to let someone else setup your listing for you, I will setup an AMAZING listing for you and have it complete within 48 hours for under $50!

Step 7: Hosting Your First Guest
Bookings, Service, Amenities and more

Here is the exciting part! Accepting bookings, hosting guest and GETTING PAID!!!!!

Service Service Service Service Service Service Service oh and did I mention SERVICE! I cannot say this enough, you have to provide EXCEPTIONAL service to your guest, it's DETRIMENTAL to your success and survival as a host to provide AMAZING service! This is where you show and prove that your pretty pictures and crafty wording aren't just talk. Service separates the Pros from the No's!

Confidence is key and the only way to be confident about hosting is preparation! Before you go live I recommend you doing a test stay in your space or having someone you know stay in your Airbnb as a guest before you go live. This will also allow you to do a test turnover the next morning so you can see how long it actually takes you to turn over your unit so that you set your check-in and check-out times according to how much time you need to get ready for your next guest. If you need a day or two in between checkouts so that the place can be turned over, you will want to set preparation times this automatically blocks either 1 or 2 nights before and after each reservation.

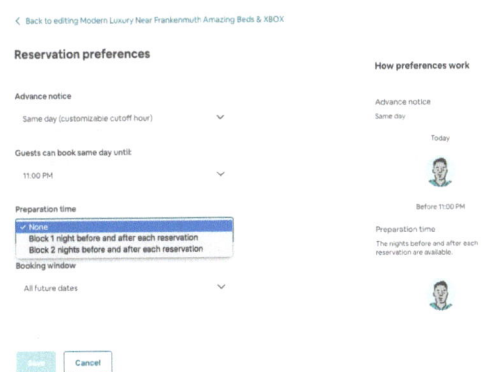

Also use your amenities list on your listing and make sure you have everything you say you will provide is available and make sure everything works! Could you imagine booking a place just because they have a washer/dryer then figure out it doesn't work when you need it most? Can we say 1 STAR RATING! We don't EVER want this to happen to us. I use 5 different pre written responses, 2 for greetings 1 for the day of check-in and 1 for the day of checkout. When I first get a booking I send my first message introducing myself, thanking them for booking with me, ask if they are celebrating any special occasions if they didn't already disclose. I do this so I can surprise and delight them upon arrival! I set expectations on what they can expect and let my guest know exactly when they will hear from me again (keeping contact from booking to checkout).

The morning of check-in I send a message within Airbnb providing them their check-in codes and instructions with a link that guides them to my check-in instructions with photos which they can also use to begin their check-in and also ask their arrival time so I am well prepared for their arrival.

On the day they checkout, I send a message that thanks them again for staying and booking with us, remind them of the checkout time, ask for feedback and then ask for a review. Keeping communication with the guest at every step of the way, keeps the guest engaged and knowing what to expect next which creates trust and reassurance that they made a good decision booking with you!

I respond to all messages and inquiries during the day and night within minutes and keep my Airbnb notifications loud because you never know when a guest may need you or have an emergency, I have yet to be awaken at night by a guest but then again I usually don't go to sleep until morning ha ha ha. Guest usually tell you why they are visiting and who will be with them . Any information I obtain I try to use as an opportunity to delight my guest but guest typically like to do their own thing and rarely need me after check-in.

Still need additional help?

Listing Creation Service and Airbnb Rental Management Services

Listing Creation Service

You will get a professionally written and edited description of your listing. Your description will include detailed information about your space, unique selling points of your Airbnb, information about the attractions nearby, house rules, 5 Pre Written Quick Responses 2 - Greetings, 1-Day of Check-in message 1-Day of Check-out message. I will also upload your professional photos and add descriptions of your photos as well.

First, Email me at Info@Jklhomesinc.com

Subject: Airbnb Listing Creation Book Offer to get your special pricing!

I will send a simple questionnaire for you to complete along with an invoice and information on how to send me your professional photos. Once you have paid your invoice, completed your questionnaire and sent photos, we will deliver a finished listing for you to review and approve within 48 hours. After your listing is complete you will then be able to go live when you are ready.

Airbnb Rental Management Services

If you are ready to start hosting but would like help planning your strategy, setting up and managing your Airbnb listing.

I offer Airbnb Rental Managing services as a Co-Host which includes: Business strategy, listing creation, and me and my team responding to all your guest inquiries and messages within minutes (Exceptional Service), getting and keeping your listing booked, gaining immediate traction and benefiting from my 5 star reviews right away.

First, Email me at: Info@Jklhomesinc.com

Subject: Airbnb Rental Managing Service Book Offer to get started!

I will send a questionnaire for you to complete, then we will schedule your free consultation to discuss your goals and see how we can serve you.

If you would like to move forward after your free consultation I will send you our Electronic Management Services Agreement. After the agreement is signed we will get started on creating the personalized strategy plan for your listing and deliver the plan via email 48 hours after our consultation.

Next we will get to work on your plan and get your space listed and booked!

Pricing is between 10%-20% of booked revenue and your first month is Free when you choose the 3-month agreement option! This gives me the opportunity to generate revenue for you BEFORE you have to pay for our service! I am incentivize to make you money or else I don't get paid!

Example: If I get your listing to generate $2,000 a month and our management agreement is 20% of booked revenue for a 3-month agreement your Airbnb Management fee to me is $0 for the first month, $400 a month thereafter.

I can virtually respond to your guest and manage your Airbnb rental only thing I cannot do is clean and turn your space over for you or physically deliver things to your guest. Everything else I have you covered. You will be in direct contact with me and you will have all access to all messages I send to your guest within your host account even with me as your co-host. You will never be out of the loop.

Thank you for reading my book! I hope you find it super helpful! And feel free to stay in touch.

Connect with me:

Facebook: @JKLhomesinc fb.me/JKLHomesInc

Instagram: @JKLhomes https://www.instagram.com/jklhomes/

Website: www.JKLhomesinc.com

Author: Nichola Dotson

Special thanks to my husband Devon my sons Jayden, Kenji and Liam!

The End

www.ingramcontent.com/pod-product-compliance
Lightning Source LLC
Chambersburg PA
CBHW042023200526
45159CB00035B/3034